Warren County MEMORIES

The Early Years • A Pictorial History

presented by

THE POST★STAR
poststar.com

ACKNOWLEDGMENTS

The Post-Star is pleased to present "Warren County Memories: The Early Years." It must be noted, however, that this unique pictorial history book would not have been possible without the generous contributions made by many people from virtually every corner of our community.

We are indebted, first of all, to those early area residents who captured their time—our history—in photographs, and provided a glimpse into their lives.

Secondly, all area residents are indebted to the many individuals who are committed to preserving our history in various libraries, historical societies, archives and personal collections throughout our community.

The following organizations have contributed greatly to this project:
Chapman Historical Museum
Crandall Public Library
Hague Historical Society
Warren County Historical Society

Published by Pediment Publishing, a division of The Pediment Group, Inc. www.pediment.com. Printed in Canada.

FOREWORD

Our area is rich in history and tradition and his pictorial book gives us a chance to take a stroll back in time in Warren County. These photographs offer a glimpse into early Warren County from the late 1800s through the 1930s. These photos capture early commerce, familiar street scenes, celebrations, and a sense of community.

We give a special thanks to our neighbors. We reached out to the community and many of you brought us your prized photographs, shared the stories of those photographs, and allowed us to include them in this book. The Chapman Historical Museum and The Folklife Center at Crandall Public Library opened their doors and willingly shared their treasures to help us create this book. Our own Maury Thompson shared some of our area's history in the chapter introductions.

We are so fortunate that our early citizens took the time to document their world with these wonderful images and so fortunate that these photographs still live in our communities.

Terry Coomes
Publisher
Post-Star

TABLE OF CONTENTS

CHAPTER ONE
VIEWS AND STREET SCENES

Tree-lined streets have long been a source of pride in Glens Falls and communities throughout Warren County.

Dutch-elm disease, which was introduced in the United States around 1930, wiped out many of the trees.

An estimated 150-year-old surviving elm tree on Upper Glen Street, near the border of Glens Falls and Queensbury, was named in 2012 to the National Register of Historic Elms.

Automobiles shared streets with horse-drawn vehicles and trolleys in the early 20th century era of transportation evolution.

Additional trolley and train runs between outlying communities and Glens Falls would be added for special occasions such as firefighter conventions and political rallies.

Enjoy these street scenes of Warren County, including a Glens Falls view looking south on Glen Street from the Rockwell House hotel, where crowds gathered in the street when President Ulysses S. Grant gave a speech on the hotel's porch during a re-election campaign swing through the region in August 1872.

OPPOSITE: Wayside Cottages, Luzerne, 1880. COURTESY CHAPMAN MUSEUM

ABOVE: A view of Warren Street, looking toward Bank Square, circa 1878.
COURTESY THE FOLKLIFE CENTER, CRANDALL PUBLIC LIBRARY, CLP-3031

RIGHT: View down the main street of Chestertown, north from the Chester Hotel, circa 1874. COURTESY CHAPMAN MUSEUM

OPPOSITE: A view of the bridge near Riverside, circa 1880. Riverside was primarily a train stop. The bridge was the highlight. Photo circa 1880.
COURTESY CHAPMAN MUSEUM

ABOVE: The fountain in front of the Rockwell House on Glen Street in the 1870s. Also visible in the photo is Reuben Peck's drug store. COURTESY THE FOLKLIFE CENTER, CRANDALL PUBLIC LIBRARY, CLP-1271

ABOVE RIGHT: A view of the east side of Glen Street, looking south from the fountain, circa 1886. COURTESY CRANDALL LIBRARY PHOTO COLLECTION

RIGHT: A view looking down Glen Street from the Soldiers' Monument, circa 1889, showing shops such as The Beehive crockery shop, Ames & Baldwin drugstore, and Whitney's & Company shoe store. COURTESY CRANDALL LIBRARY PHOTO COLLECTION

ABOVE: The road to Bolton, Lake George, circa 1880. Included in this view is the summer place of H.H. Hayden. The cottage was burned down in 1909. COURTESY CHAPMAN MUSEUM

LEFT: A view looking south down Glen Street from the Rockwell House, Glens Falls, circa 1880. COURTESY CHAPMAN MUSEUM

ABOVE: A view of Glen Street from the south in 1889.
COURTESY CRANDALL LIBRARY PHOTO COLLECTION

ABOVE RIGHT: A view of the Soldier's Monument, looking east, circa 1900. COURTESY THE FOLKLIFE CENTER, CRANDALL PUBLIC LIBRARY, CLP-2505

RIGHT: A view looking up the Hudson River in the 1880s.
COURTESY THE FOLKLIFE CENTER, CRANDALL PUBLIC LIBRARY, CLP-1665

ABOVE: A view of Ridge Street, circa 1905.
COURTESY THE FOLKLIFE CENTER, CRANDALL PUBLIC LIBRARY, CLP-OV-120

LEFT: A bustling Glen Street in the late 1800s with a horse-drawn sleigh.
COURTESY THE FOLKLIFE CENTER, CRANDALL PUBLIC LIBRARY, CLP-2146

ABOVE: A view of Glens Falls as seen from South Glens Falls, looking across the Iron Bridge, circa 1905.
COURTESY THE FOLKLIFE CENTER, CRANDALL PUBLIC LIBRARY, CLP-OV-18

RIGHT: A view looking north up Glen Street with Warren Street at right, circa 1905.
COURTESY THE FOLKLIFE CENTER, CRANDALL PUBLIC LIBRARY, CLP-2178

OPPOSITE TOP LEFT: The Burge Block in Chestertown, circa 1906. The building on the corner served as the town's post office and the upper floor housed the Chestertown Telephone Company, started by Charles Burge and others in the late 1800s. Standing at left of the building are Charles Burge, Marion Burge, Mrs. Burge and Esther Burge.
COURTESY JOHN JANSSEN

OPPOSITE TOP RIGHT: View of a trolley on snow-covered Glen and Warren Streets in Glens Falls, circa 1905. COURTESY CHAPMAN MUSEUM

OPPOSITE BOTTOM: A view of Glen Street, circa 1905.
COURTESY POSTCARD COLLECTION,
THE FOLKLIFE CENTER, CRANDALL PUBLIC LIBRARY

ABOVE: A view of the Hudson River with Glens Falls at left, including the Finch, Pruyn & Co. newspaper mills in the distance. COURTESY THE FOLKLIFE CENTER, CRANDALL PUBLIC LIBRARY, CLP-OV-19

LEFT: A bustling downtown Glens Falls, circa 1912. COURTESY CHAPMAN MUSEUM

OPPOSITE BOTTOM LEFT: Hague village center in 1910 (today's intersection of Route 9N and Route 8). The building at left housed the barber shop and bowling alley, while the building in the center of the photo is the Hillside Hotel. The boat is the Uncas, built in Jesse Sexton's shop for hotelier and businessman Smith Sexton, and launched in 1910. It could hold up to 30 passengers, transporting them to and from hotels along the lake. COURTESY TOWN OF HAGUE HISTORICAL ARCHIVES

OPPOSITE BOTTOM RIGHT: Site of the new bridge over the Schroon River and houses beyond. October 20, 1933. COURTESY CHAPMAN MUSEUM

CHAPTER TWO

TRANSPORTATION

Bicycle and walking trails have replaced many of the railroad tracks that once ran through Warren County.

Highways have replaced stagecoach routes.

Modern transportation infrastructure is designed primarily for individuals instead of group travel.

Tractor-trailers have replaced canal boats as the primary mode of transporting locally manufactured goods to market.

In the mid-1960s, state Sen. Nathan Proller, R-Glens Falls, spearheaded construction of a highway to the top of Prospect Mountain in Lake George, a route once traveled by cable railroad.

Tour boats on Lake George are a nostalgic reminder of historic steamboats, such as the one Thomas Jefferson traveled on in 1791, when he wrote to his daughter, "Lake George is, without comparison, the most beautiful water I ever saw."

Enjoy these views of historic transportation in Warren County.

OPPOSITE: Railroad train engine No. 1618 of the NYNH&H with worker and young boy standing in foreground. COURTESY CHAPMAN MUSEUM

ABOVE: View of the Hudson River and Adirondack Railroad near the Glen, circa 1880. COURTESY CHAPMAN MUSEUM

RIGHT: View of the Adirondack Railroad Bridge across the Sacandaga River at Luzerne, circa 1880. COURTESY CHAPMAN MUSEUM

ABOVE: Glens Falls Train Depot on Maple Street, circa 1875. COURTESY CHAPMAN MUSEUM

ABOVE LEFT: View of the Adirondack Railroad station at Thurman, circa 1880. COURTESY CHAPMAN MUSEUM

LEFT: A coach in front of the North River Hotel in Johnsburg, circa 1880. COURTESY CHAPMAN MUSEUM

ABOVE: Stagecoach at the Adirondack Railroad depot in North Creek, circa 1880. COURTESY CHAPMAN MUSEUM

ABOVE RIGHT: Joseph Mills in his elk-drawn wagon in front of the Presbyterian Church, circa 1890.
COURTESY THE FOLKLIFE CENTER, CRANDALL PUBLIC LIBRARY, CLP-1322

RIGHT: The Adirondack Railroad travelled from Saratoga Springs to North Creek through Luzerne, Riverside, Chestertown, Schroon Lake, Root's, and North Creek. Photo circa 1880. COURTESY CHAPMAN MUSEUM

ABOVE: View of an Adirondack Railroad train by the Hudson River in the early 1880s. COURTESY CHAPMAN MUSEUM

ABOVE LEFT: The steamer Ganouskie being boarded at a dock at Bolton on Lake George, circa 1880. COURTESY CHAPMAN MUSEUM

LEFT: Excursion steamer on Lake George in the 1880s. COURTESY THE FOLKLIFE CENTER, CRANDALL PUBLIC LIBRARY, CLP-42

ABOVE: William E. Spier in his horse-drawn sleigh in the late 1800s.

COURTESY THE FOLKLIFE CENTER, CRANDALL PUBLIC LIBRARY, CLP-1880

ABOVE RIGHT: Glens Falls, Sandy Hill & Fort Edward Street Railroad Company at 51 Feeder Road in Hudson Falls, circa 1890.

COURTESY CHAPMAN MUSEUM

RIGHT: A horse-drawn carriage on a rural road in Warren County, circa 1890.

COURTESY RACHEL CLOTHIER

ABOVE: Cable railroad on Prospect Mountain, circa 1890. COURTESY CHAPMAN MUSEUM

LEFT: Engine No. 147 at the Glens Falls Railroad Station, late 1800s.
COURTESY THE FOLKLIFE CENTER, CRANDALL PUBLIC LIBRARY, CLP-1412

ABOVE: A stagecoach approaches the toll gate near Lake George, above the Halfway House, circa 1880. COURTESY THE FOLKLIFE CENTER, CRANDALL PUBLIC LIBRARY, CLP-96

RIGHT: Steel bridge across the Hudson River at Glens Falls, looking north. COURTESY THE FOLKLIFE CENTER, CRANDALL PUBLIC LIBRARY, CLP-1666

OPPOSITE: Stagecoaches carrying guests prepare to approach the tollgate in Queensbury in the late 1800s. Travelers often journeyed by stagecoach from the American Hotel in Glens Falls to the steamship dock in Caldwell. Once there, they would travel by boat to hotels on the lake that were accessible only by water travel. COURTESY ANDREW HOLDING

ABOVE: A street-level view of the construction of the trolley lines for the Hudson Valley Railroad Company at Bank Square in Glens Falls, circa 1909. COURTESY CHAPMAN MUSEUM

RIGHT: Railroad Station at Lake George, circa 1905.
COURTESY CHAPMAN MUSEUM

ABOVE: Horse-drawn carriages in front of the Queensbury home of Stephen and Emma Thomas, circa 1900s. Built in 1890, it was 200 feet long and included 70 cow stations, 10 horse stalls, and 6 bedrooms. The home burned to the ground on Christmas Eve, 1915. COURTESY PATRICIA PORTER

ABOVE LEFT: John Jenkins (1860-1930) at the cider mill, located on Route 8, less than a mile from the center of Hague. Jenkins liked to end a hard day of work with a nip or two of hard cider. He owned and operated a carriage company, which also included the operation of a stage coach line between Hague and Ticonderoga. He also owned and operated a local meat market and grocery store, and held several local elected positions, including Superintendent of Highways for the town. COURTESY TOWN OF HAGUE HISTORICAL ARCHIVES

LEFT: Laying the "passing switch" for the electric trolley system in 1898. COURTESY THE FOLKLIFE CENTER, CRANDALL PUBLIC LIBRARY, CLP-1134

ABOVE: Martin L. C. Wilmarth in his first car, a blue Buick, pauses in front of 3 Culvert Street in Glens Falls, 1910. COURTESY ANDREW HOLDING

ABOVE LEFT: Canal boat in the feeder canal, circa 1910.
COURTESY THE FOLKLIFE CENTER, CRANDALL PUBLIC LIBRARY, CLP-1680

LEFT: Early automobile in front of the Empire Automobile Company in Glens Falls, circa 1908. Behind the wheel is Daniel H. Cowles and in the front seat next to him is Frank Starbuck. In the back seat, from left, are Ed Angel, James Reynolds and L.M. Brown.
COURTESY THE FOLKLIFE CENTER, CRANDALL PUBLIC LIBRARY, CLP-280

OPPOSITE: People boarding the Horicon on Lake George, circa 1910.
COURTESY CHAPMAN MUSEUM

ABOVE: Men and women examining a plane at Aviation Field (later Floyd Bennett Field), circa 1915. COURTESY CHAPMAN MUSEUM

LEFT: Cement Barge on Feeder Canal, circa 1920. COURTESY WARREN COUNTY HISTORICAL SOCIETY, FROM FRANCIS BAAYLE

OPPOSITE TOP: Prospect Mountain Railway in the early 1900s. COURTESY WARREN COUNTY HISTORICAL SOCIETY

OPPOSITE BOTTOM LEFT: Employees in front of the D&H Freight Office in Glens Falls, circa 1914. COURTESY THE FOLKLIFE CENTER, CRANDALL PUBLIC LIBRARY, CLP-1188

OPPOSITE BOTTOM RIGHT: Hague road crew in the early 1900s. When cars first arrived on the scene, roads were not yet paved. The highway crews put planks down on the roads to keep these vehicles from getting stuck in the mud. Mud season – the Adirondacks' fifth season – still today causes many smaller roads in town to be closed to vehicles over a certain weight. COURTESY TOWN OF HAGUE HISTORICAL ARCHIVES

CHAPTER THREE

SCHOOLS AND EDUCATION

Athletics and music have long been a part of the education system in Warren County.

Education has evolved from systems of small one-room and two-room schools to consolidated districts.

In Queensbury, 11 schools consolidated to form Queensbury Union Free School District in 1948.

The new district opened a high school that had its first graduating class in 1953.

In the late 19th and early 20th centuries, many area youths attended private high schools.

Glens Falls Academy, which opened in 1803, closed in 1937.

St. Mary's Academy, now St. Mary's- St. Alphonsus Regional Catholic School, stopped offering high school classes in 1989.

The infrastructure of education has changed, but the excitement of learning stays the same.

Enjoy these historic photos of schools in Warren County.

OPPOSITE: Students of the "Institute" in front of the Warren County Court House, 1868. COURTESY THE FOLKLIFE CENTER, CRANDALL PUBLIC LIBRARY, CLP-112

ABOVE: Glens Falls High School students, circa 1890. Seated on the ground, from left: Louis Armstrong, Harry Palmet, Lizzie Briggs, Lulu Ferguson, Pauline Eddy, Augusta Silver, D.J. Eddy. Second row, from left: Louis McDonald, Beecher Allen, Gertrude Eddy, Nellie Farmer, Alexa Beaudoin, Stella White, Nettie Hartman. Back row, from left: Harry Cronkhite, George Scott, Clayton Barber, William Lennov, Arhur Wait, Louis Chitty, Walter Lapham, Ernest Ames, Bertha Wait, S. Williams, Lillian Pearsall, Lillian Potter, Herbert Finch, Annabel Beaudoin, R. DeLong, Gertrude Ferguson. COURTESY THE FOLKLIFE CENTER, CRANDALL PUBLIC LIBRARY, CLP-114

RIGHT: Glens Falls Academy students in 1884. Seated, from left are: Bertha Rockwell and Mary Pruyn Hoopes. Standing from left are: Lillian Pearsall, Sophie Rogers Johnson, Mable Rogers and Aline Cleveland.
COURTESY CRANDALL LIBRARY PHOTO COLLECTION

OPPOSITE TOP: Glens Falls Academy students and faculty, circa 1900.
COURTESY THE FOLKLIFE CENTER, CRANDALL PUBLIC LIBRARY, CLP-OV-93

OPPOSITE BOTTOM LEFT: A group of children in front of the West Mountain School, Also known as the Gurney Lane School, late 1800s COURTESY CHAPMAN MUSEUM

OPPOSITE BOTTOM RIGHT: Glens Falls Academy students and faculty in front of their school on Warren Street in the late 1800s. COURTESY THE FOLKLIFE CENTER, CRANDALL PUBLIC LIBRARY, CLP-446

ABOVE: Union School No. 1 at the corner of Glen and Union streets in the 1890s. This school was used as Glen Falls High School and burned on December 17, 1902. COURTESY THE FOLKLIFE CENTER, CRANDALL PUBLIC LIBRARY, CLP-2205

ABOVE RIGHT: Chestertown school students in the early 1900s. COURTESY JOHN JANSSEN

RIGHT: One of several schools in Hague at that time, this building was at the intersection of Route 9N and Split Rock Road and served the South Hague School District. The various Hague school districts were consolidated into the Hague Central School District in 1927, and a single, larger school was built to serve the entire community. In 1979, Hague Central School District was annexed by the Ticonderoga School District and the school building was no longer used. Today, the Hague Community Center sits on the site where that school once was. COURTESY TOWN OF HAGUE HISTORICAL ARCHIVES

ABOVE: South Street School students. Identified are Hira Wells, Bill Hortin, Walt Garret, Harry Whelin, Day Hortin, Wallis See, George Riandim, Ernest Bur, Byron Martine, Hugh Harillin, Charlie Clark, Jim Hogan, Ira Casavak, Miss Bunker and Arnold Thomas.
COURTESY THE FOLKLIFE CENTER, CRANDALL PUBLIC LIBRARY, CLP-1914

LEFT: Students in front of the Boulevard School, Queensbury School District school no. 2, 1880s. COURTESY CHAPMAN MUSEUM

ABOVE: Unknown event in front of Glens Falls High School, circa 1905.
COURTESY CRANDALL LIBRARY PHOTO COLLECTION

ABOVE RIGHT: Glens Falls Academy baseball team, circa 1907.
COURTESY THE FOLKLIFE CENTER, CRANDALL PUBLIC LIBRARY, CLP-156

RIGHT: The 1905 Glens Falls High School football team.
COURTESY CHAPMAN MUSEUM

OPPOSITE: Ridge Street School nature study class at Cole's Wood, circa 1906. COURTESY THE FOLKLIFE CENTER, CRANDALL PUBLIC LIBRARY, CLP-1944

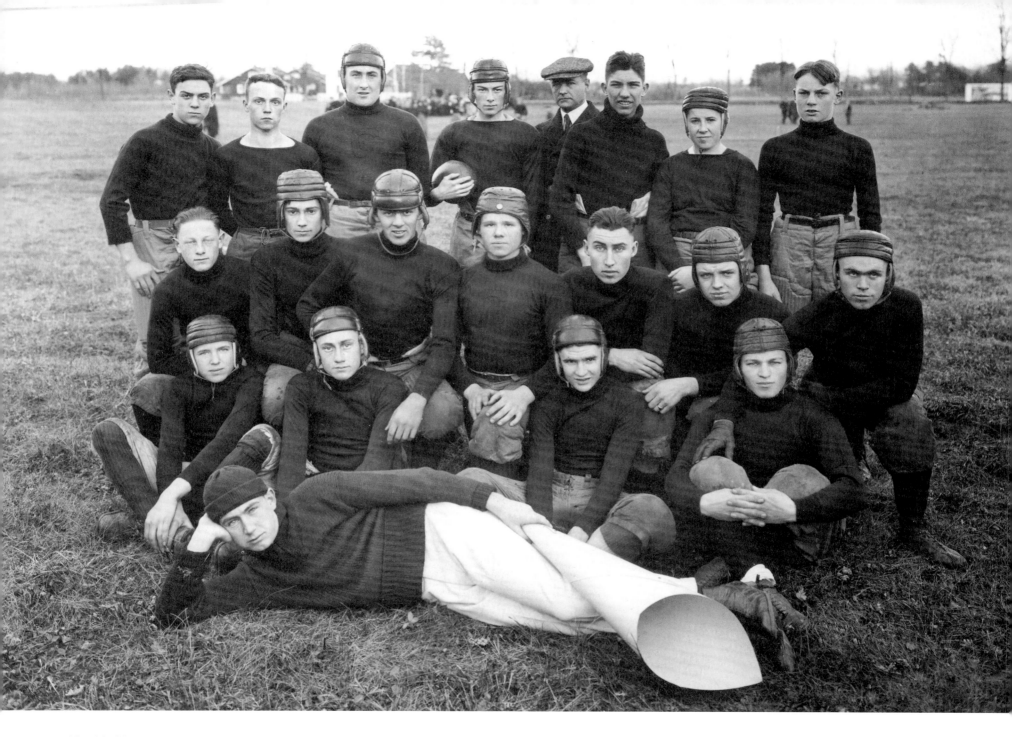

LEFT: Professor Clark and other teachers in front of Luzerne High School, circa 1915. COURTESY CHAPMAN MUSEUM

OPPOSITE: Glens Falls High School football team of 1918. COURTESY THE FOLKLIFE CENTER, CRANDALL PUBLIC LIBRARY, CLP-781

BELOW LEFT: Glens Falls High School basketball team, league champions in 1911 and 1912. COURTESY CHAPMAN MUSEUM

BELOW: Elementary students at Warrensburg School in 1917. Identified are, back row: Stine, Margaret Stone, Lawrence Parker, Shaw, unidentified, Ernest N, Edward Harrington, DeRay Dickinson, Preston Sjragne. Second Row: Miles, Marg Hall, Franklin Wheeler, Frank Reignold, Hugh Maeier, Evelyn Brown, William Cleever, Beulah Dinkley. Third Row: Theron Drake, Hilda Shaw, Clayton Bolton, Madeline Fuller, Julie Morjihan, Edna Brainand, Masie B, Arikin Sojer Woodward. COURTESY THE FOLKLIFE CENTER, CRANDALL PUBLIC LIBRARY, CLP-2863

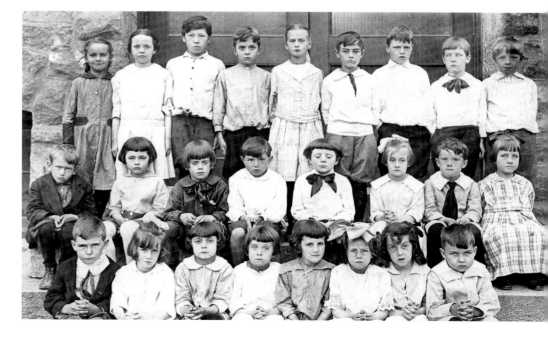

ABOVE: St. Mary's Academy Catholic School on the corner of Warren Street and Church Street, Glens Falls, 1920s. At the time, St. Mary's was the largest parochial school in the country.
COURTESY ANN-MARIE WOLCOTT

ABOVE RIGHT: Glens Falls Academy class of 1931.
COURTESY CHAPMAN MUSEUM

RIGHT: Laying the corner stone for Jackson Heights School in 1936. Mr. Charles McLaughlin, center right, standing on the ground, is speaking and on his left is Mrs. Sara Lawrence, the school's principal. Directly above McLaughlin are board of education members, from left: Judge J. Ward Russell, M. L. Carson, Alpha Barber, Powel J. Smith, Robert S. Buddy, William H. Barber, Frank Conlin, and Superintendent of Schools Alexander W. Miller.
COURTESY CHAPMAN MUSEUM

OPPOSITE: The Glens Falls High School girls field hockey team, circa 1928. COURTESY CHAPMAN MUSEUM

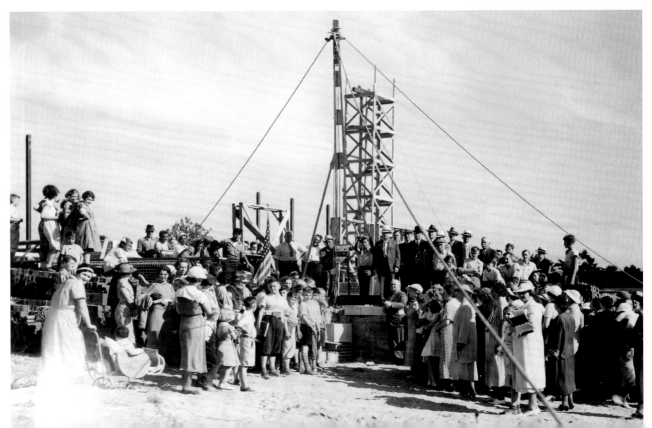

CHAPTER FOUR

COMMERCE AND INDUSTRY

You won't find factory employees in Warren County today working barefoot. But many of the county's historic industries still operate, in some cases under different corporate ownership.

Finch, Pruyn & Co., now Finch Paper, still makes paper at its mill on Glen Street in Glens Falls.

The Morning Star, established in 1883, merged with *The Morning Post* in 1909 to become *The Post-Star*, which still publishes the news of Warren County daily in print and up to the minute on poststar.com.

Lime is still quarried and cement still manufactured at Jointa Galusha and Lehigh Hanson facilities on Warren Street in Glens Falls.

The garment industry is an exception to the norm.

A few dozen garment factories once operated in Warren County.

Native Textiles on Warren Street, the last garment factory in Glens Falls, closed in 2005.

The lodging industry has evolved from the historic hotels of the early 20th century to roadside motels and cabin colonies of mid-century and now primarily modern multi-story hotels in Queensbury and Lake George.

Enjoy these views of historic industry and commerce in Warren County.

OPPOSITE: Displays and workers at Woolworth's Store on Glen Street, circa 1930. COURTESY CHAPMAN MUSEUM

ABOVE: Glens Falls, Lime Works, from below the bridge, showing offices, cooperage and storage buildings, circa 1880. COURTESY CHAPMAN MUSEUM

OPPOSITE: The Fort William Henry Hotel on Lake George in the 1880s.
COURTESY THE FOLKLIFE CENTER, CRANDALL PUBLIC LIBRARY, CLP-92

BELOW: View of the main building at the Rockwell Hotel in Lake Luzerne, circa 1880. COURTESY CHAPMAN MUSEUM

ABOVE: Hubbell Sawmill, Lake George circa 1888.
COURTESY MARGARET MANNIX, HISTORIAN FOR LAKE GEORGE

ABOVE LEFT: A Rochester Clothing Store delivery wagon driver stops to talk with a boy with a wagon pulled by a donkey, 1890. COURTESY CHAPMAN MUSEUM

LEFT: Men and children standing in front of the Coolidge and Bentley store on Glen Street, circa 1885. In the windows are signs for the "Grand Pumpkin Pie Carnival, Sept. 16th." Piles of large pumpkins are in front of store windows. Upstairs is the M.B. Little Insurance Co. office.
COURTESY CHAPMAN MUSEUM

OPPOSITE: Stage coaches in front of Ft. William Henry Hotel on Lake George, circa 1890.
COURTESY THE FOLKLIFE CENTER, CRANDALL PUBLIC LIBRARY, CLP-2276

ABOVE: View of the Wayside Inn's office, with three men at desks, Lake Luzerne, 1885. The Wayside Inn sat on the site of the present day high school. COURTESY CHAPMAN MUSEUM

ABOVE RIGHT: Owner William Frederick Gubitz binding books at W.F. Gubitz Book Bindery and Paper Ruling, Glens Falls, 1894. William is the grandfather of Lois Gubitz Clements and the great-grandfather of Brian Clements and Susan Clements Kozak. COURTESY BRIAN CLEMENTS AND SUSAN CLEMENTS KOZAK.

RIGHT: The interior of the O. C. Smith store, 5 Crandall Block (178 Glen St.), Glens Falls, circa 1895. COURTESY CHAPMAN MUSEUM

ABOVE: Store employees standing in front of Chas A. Hovey fruit market in Glens Falls, circa 1895. COURTESY CHAPMAN MUSEUM

LEFT: Oxen pulling logs out of the woods in the snow, near Route 8 in the Hague area, late 1800s. Logging was one of the major industries in Hague for many decades in the 19th and early 20th centuries. Loggers would bring the logs down to the lake in the winter, where they laid in wait until the lake thawed. Two chutes in Hague – one near today's Trout House Village and one near Jenkins Brook – were used to put the logs into the water. From there, they were floated to Ticonderoga for use in the paper mill or to be transported to other destinations. COURTESY TOWN OF HAGUE HISTORICAL ARCHIVES

ABOVE: Beilman Tannery at Stony Creek, circa 1895. Seated fifth from right is Clifford Denno. COURTESY CHAPMAN MUSEUM

LEFT: Graphite was mined in Hague starting in 1887. Many of the workers were immigrants, recruited on the docks of New York City. A group of Polish mine workers in Hague is shown here. A popular local story recounts the discovery of this mineral in Hague by Sam Ackerman, who owned a farm in West Hague. He recognized the telltale greasy smear that spread across the snow in the wake of a log he was hauling from the woods. During the heyday of the mines, the settlement known as Graphite included a boarding house, stores, a school, a theater, three bars, and a poolroom as well as numerous homes. The huge crushing mill produced an ore averaging 70 percent graphite. This material was transported by horse and wagon four miles down the mountain to the lake, loaded onto boats, and shipped to Baldwin Dock in Ticonderoga, where it was then transported to the mill downtown. There, it was refined to produce 99 percent pure graphite powder. Costs, combined with growing labor unrest, brought an end to the mining operations in 1921. This area of Hague is still known today as Graphite. COURTESY TOWN OF HAGUE HISTORICAL ARCHIVES

ABOVE: Graphite was also mined at a site close to the shores of Lake George. These mines were known as the Lakeshore Mines.
COURTESY TOWN OF HAGUE HISTORICAL ARCHIVES

ABOVE LEFT: Moore and Starbuck Market on Main Street in Luzerne, 1890s
COURTESY CHAPMAN MUSEUM

ABOVE: Workmen at the nearly completed Foulds house on Ridge Street, circa 1894.
COURTESY CHAPMAN MUSEUM

ABOVE LEFT: Interior view of a printing workshop in Glens Falls, circa 1895.
COURTESY CHAPMAN MUSEUM

LEFT: View of the yard of the Finch, Pruyn & Co. sawmill located upstream of the bridge over the Hudson River near where Mohican Street is now, circa late 1800s.
COURTESY FREDERIC CHASE

OPPOSITE: Kendrick and Brown Company workers, Lawrence Street, Glens Falls, circa 1898.
COURTESY CHAPMAN MUSEUM

ABOVE: Workers dredging the Feeder Canal in Glens Falls, circa 1890. In the back ground is a lime kiln. COURTESY CHAPMAN MUSEUM

LEFT: View of a riverman guiding a raft of logs through a channel on the river above the falls, circa 1880. COURTESY CHAPMAN MUSEUM

OPPOSITE: Varney Brothers flour, feed and grain store at 27 South Street in Glens Falls, circa 1900. The store was in business circa 1892-1942. COURTESY CHAPMAN MUSEUM

ABOVE: Opera House on Warren
Street in Glens Falls, circa 1900.

ABOVE RIGHT: Red Line Fruit Company, located in
Glens Falls, was owned by Martin J. Callahan, circa
1900.

RIGHT: View of logs above the Spier Falls dam on the
Hudson River after a spring flood that interrupted
construction, circa 1901.

OPPOSITE: Men at work clearing the river bed of
sediment during construction of the Spier Falls
Dam, circa 1902.

ABOVE: Employees working at the Morning Star, circa 1905.

RIGHT: Construction work underway on the expansion of the Finch, Pruyn & Co. mill, circa 1903.

ABOVE: Employees of the Morning Post, in front of their building, circa 1905. COURTESY CHAPMAN MUSEUM

ABOVE LEFT: The first Wilmarth Furniture delivery truck in Glens Falls, 1908. Wilmarth furniture was located on Ridge Street in downtown Glens Falls. COURTESY ANDREW HOLDING

LEFT: Barton and Keenan Market, shown here in a photo taken by the Sexton sisters (Flora and Theresa) in the very early 1900s. Originally built as a general store by Ellis Bolton, this market is today the oldest continuously operating general store in the Adirondacks. The name was later changed to Keenan Brothers Store and to The Hague Super Market in 1949, when it was purchased by Bob and Ada Hoyt. It is located on Route 8 in the center of Hague, and is known today as The Hague Market. Third from right in the photo is James Fitzgerald, great-grandfather of Sally De Larm Rypkema, who today owns the market with her husband, Jim. COURTESY TOWN OF HAGUE HISTORICAL ARCHIVES

ABOVE: Collecting sap for maple syrup on Battle Hill Road in Hague in the early 1900s. Maple syrup was made by Hague residents from the very early days of the town. In fact, maple sugar and maple syrup were the main sources of income for Wardboro, a section of Hague that included Tongue Mountain and part of Graphite. Each year, in late winter, maple trees were tapped and buckets hung on the trees to collect the sap. The sap flows when temperatures fall below freezing at night and rise above freezing during the day. When the sap was running, the sap buckets were checked every day and emptied into barrels, which were pulled on a sleigh by horses to the sugar house. There, it was boiled over a wood fire to make maple syrup. It takes 40 gallons of sap to make one gallon of syrup. The syrup can be boiled down further to produce maple sugar, with one gallon of syrup producing eight pounds of sugar. Today, maple sugaring operations in Hague still use these old-fashioned methods of collection and boiling. COURTESY TOWN OF HAGUE HISTORICAL ARCHIVES

RIGHT: The Collins House, circa early 1900s. COURTESY FREDERIC CHASE

ABOVE: A local barber shop serving men in the Glens Falls community, circa early 1900s. Barber Jeremiah Dyke Lynch is pictured fourth man from left. COURTESY ANN-MARIE WOLCOTT

LEFT: Newman Peabody in front of his hotel on the east side of Glen Street in the early 1900s. COURTESY THE FOLKLIFE CENTER, CRANDALL PUBLIC LIBRARY, CLP-1127

BELOW: The bar at Peabody's Hotel in the early 1900s. Proprietor Newman Peabody is at far right. COURTESY THE FOLKLIFE CENTER, CRANDALL PUBLIC LIBRARY, CLP-1126

ABOVE: Panoramic view northeast to southeast of the Glens Falls Dam under construction, September 15, 1913. COURTESY LIBRARY OF CONGRESS, HAER NY,57-GLEFA,1--19

LEFT: Telephone company workers repairing the line over the Hudson River between Glens Falls and South Glens Falls after the flood of 1913. COURTESY CHAPMAN MUSEUM

OPPOSITE BOTTOM LEFT: Finch, Pruyn & Co. mill, circa 1910. COURTESY THE FOLKLIFE CENTER, CRANDALL PUBLIC LIBRARY, CLP-819

OPPOSITE BOTTOM RIGHT: The laundry for the Hillside Hotel, early 1900s. The five women working in the laundry washed and ironed the linens for the hotel's dining room as well as the guests' linens and towels. The water and the flatirons were heated on a wood stove, shown in the photo. One can only imagine the heat that these laundresses had to endure on those hot summer days. COURTESY TOWN OF HAGUE HISTORICAL ARCHIVES

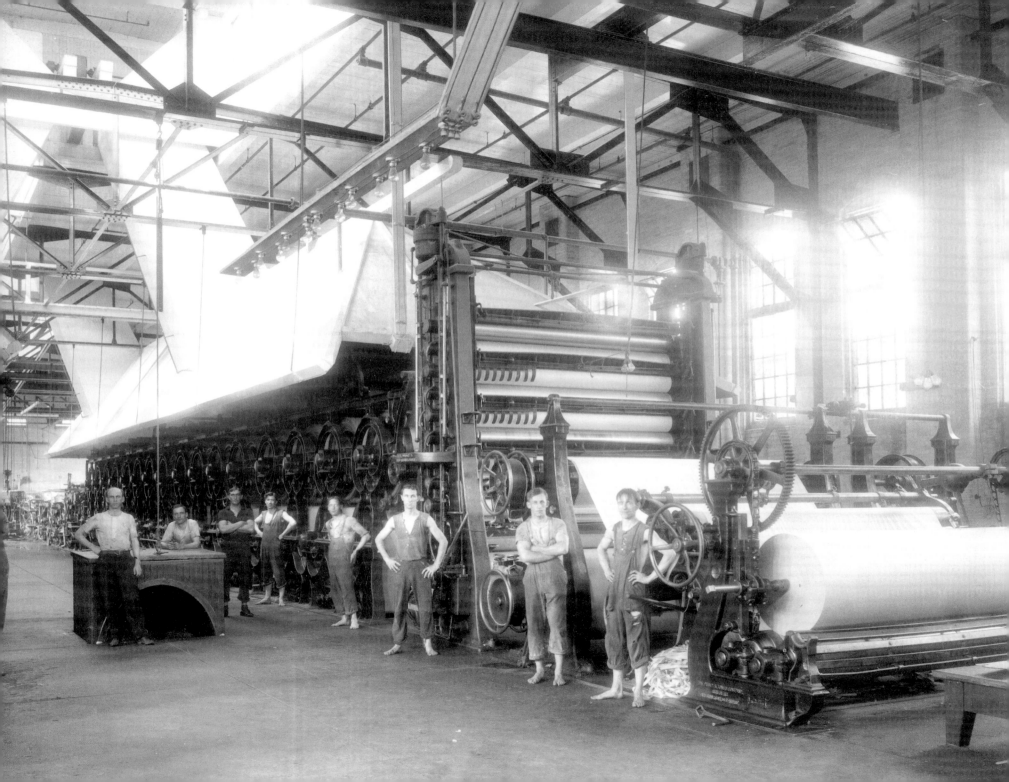

ABOVE: The Griffing and Leland Company office, circa 1914.
COURTESY THE FOLKLIFE CENTER, CRANDALL PUBLIC LIBRARY, CLP-1133

ABOVE LEFT: Charles Burge in his office at the Chestertown Phone Company in the 1920s. COURTESY JOHN JANSSEN

LEFT: Moving the second Glens Falls Insurance Company building, circa 1911. COURTESY CHAPMAN MUSEUM

OPPOSITE: Interior of Finch, Pruyn & Co. mill in the early 1900s. COURTESY THE FOLKLIFE CENTER, CRANDALL PUBLIC LIBRARY, CLP-1137

ABOVE: J.B. Cooper of Diamond Point is the passenger in this truck owned by his construction company in the 1920s. Cooper was the general contractor in charge of the construction work on the Sagamore Golf Club House and Golf Course on Federal Hill which was completed in 1928. COURTESY JACK HARVEY

ABOVE RIGHT: Interior of the Clark Glove Factory in Glens Falls, circa 1924. The young lady behind the counter is identified as Bertha De Vol. COURTESY NANCY DE VOL

RIGHT: Automotive supplies line the shelves at Empire Auto, located on Grand Street in Glens Falls, 1924. COURTESY STEPHEN AND ANDREA MATTE

OPPOSITE LEFT / OPPOSITE TOP RIGHT: Street view of Empire Auto, located on Grand Street in Glens Falls, 1924. COURTESY STEPHEN AND ANDREA MATTE

OPPOSITE BOTTOM RIGHT: William George Janssen, a wallpaper designer for Imperial Wallpaper in Glens Falls in the 1920s. COURTESY JOHN JANSSEN

ABOVE: A view inside of Empire Auto's repair facility, located on Grand Street in Glens Falls, 1924. COURTESY STEPHEN AND ANDREA MATTE

ABOVE RIGHT: Inside the Bohrer and Donohue Bakery, located on the corner of Lawrence Street and Walnut Street in Glens Falls, 1929. From left are Regina Bohrer and Frances Bohrer. COURTESY ANN-MARIE WOLCOTT

RIGHT: Personnel inside Eagle Clothing Company on Glen Street, circa 1925. COURTESY CHAPMAN MUSEUM

OPPOSITE: Hard at work in the Bohrer and Donohue Bakery, located on the corner of Lawrence Street and Walnut Street in Glens Falls, 1929. From left is owner Conrad Bohrer, owner Daniel Donohue, two unidentified men, and Frances Bohrer. COURTESY ANN-MARIE WOLCOTT

ABOVE: Group of employees of Merkel & Gelman, in the Crocheting and Weaving department, circa 1935. COURTESY CHAPMAN MUSEUM

ABOVE LEFT: George S. Hood standing beside his delivery truck for the Adirondack Dairy Company for whom he worked, circa 1925. COURTESY NANCY DE VOL

LEFT: Exterior of McMullen Leavens Co. on Cooper and Lawrence Streets, Glens Falls, circa 1929. COURTESY CHAPMAN MUSEUM

OPPOSITE: Sewing Room at McMullen Leavens Factory, Glens Falls, late 1930s. COURTESY CHAPMAN MUSEUM

CHAPTER FIVE

COMMUNITY

Crandall Public Library and Crandall Park, where he and his wife are buried, bear the name of Henry Crandall.

But little is known today about the lives of members of the Boys Savings Club, which the lumber baron, real estate investor and philanthropist founded.

One hundred boys opened savings accounts and met regularly to learn about values of work ethic, temperance and savings.

Any boy who saved $37.50 by age 21 would receive $62.50 from Crandall, bringing the total nest egg to $100.

Crandall is emblematic of the community spirit that has long been prevalent in Warren County, even in times of economic woe.

Many Warren County natives accomplished great things, including two that served as New York governors.

John Alden Dix, a Democrat, was governor in 1911 and 1912.

Dix, in 1904, was co-founder of *The Morning Post*, a Glens Falls daily newspaper that merged with *The Morning Star* in 1909 to become *The Post-Star*.

Charles Evans Hughes, a Republican, was governor from 1907 to Oct. 6, 1910, when he resigned to accept appointment to the U.S. Supreme Court.

Enjoy these historic photographs that show the community spirit of Warren County.

OPPOSITE: Cold Water Club on Glen Island, Lake George, September 1892. Back row: A. Newton Locke; William McEachron; Mr. Whipple; Seated: James Clarke; Jerome Lapham; B.F. Lapham; Jabina Ellis; Fred Johnson; Orange Ferris. COURTESY CHAPMAN MUSEUM

ABOVE: Priests studying in the Common Room of the Priests' House at St. Mary's of the Lake, the summer home of the Paulist Fathers, in Lake George, 1876. COURTESY PAULIST FATHERS

ABOVE RIGHT: The Paulist House, Lake George, 1876. Built in 1875 by Father Isaac Hecker, C.S.P., the house served as a residence for Paulist Priests. COURTESY PAULIST FATHERS

RIGHT: A group of youngsters dressed in military garb, circa 1870s. COURTESY THE FOLKLIFE CENTER, CRANDALL PUBLIC LIBRARY, CLP-115

OPPOSITE: Ranger family and guests at the Summer Rest landing on Ranger Island, circa 1879. COURTESY CHAPMAN MUSEUM

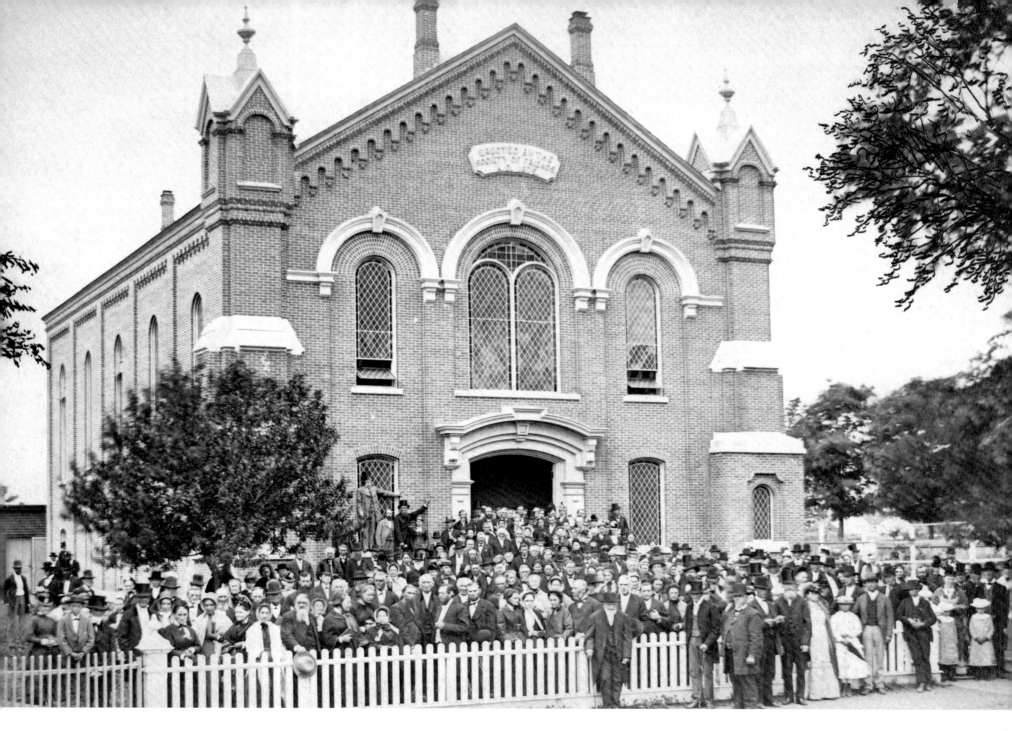

ABOVE: The Sullivan family farmhouse in Queensbury, circa late 1800s. COURTESY CAROL A. PARROTT

ABOVE LEFT: Patrick Sullivan, his wife Ellen Scannell, and their eight children, on the front step of their farm in Highland, circa late 1800s. The farm, handed down to Patrick and John Sullivan, became Sullivan's Dairy. COURTESY CAROL A. PARROTT

LEFT: Church of St. Sacrement, Bolton, circa 1870. COURTESY CHAPMAN MUSEUM

OPPOSITE: The Society of Friends Meeting, Ridge Street, Glens Falls, June 5, 1878. COURTESY CHAPMAN MUSEUM

ABOVE: Patrick Sullivan and his wife, Ellen, sitting outside their farmhouse in Queensbury, circa late 1800s. COURTESY CAROL A. PARROTT

RIGHT: View of the Church of the Holy Cross in Warrensburg, circa 1880. COURTESY CHAPMAN MUSEUM

ABOVE: A view of the St. Mary's Summer Camp across Lake George, circa early 1900s. The boathouse and the caretaker's house are along the shore, while the priests' house and the north wing of the students' house are located just behind them.
COURTESY PAULIST FATHERS

ABOVE LEFT: The Massiano family in front of their home at 53-55 Cooper Street in Glens Falls, circa 1900. From left, James Massiano, son Michael F., daughter Carmella, daughter Josephine, wife Rosa.
COURTESY MICHAEL F. MASSIANO, JR.

LEFT: Michael F. Massiano, Jr. on the steps of the home of his grandparents Frank and Mary Orsini at 56 Walnut Street, 6F, circa 1900. At left is a sign on Poopie's Restaurant.
COURTESY MICHAEL F. MASSIANO, JR.

ABOVE: Glens Falls Club in front of the Empire Theatre, circa 1900.
COURTESY THE FOLKLIFE CENTER, CRANDALL PUBLIC LIBRARY, CLP-1866

RIGHT: The Lynch family pauses for a family photo at their home on Madison Street in Glens Falls, 1902. Front row, from left are brothers Francis Bartholomew Lynch and J. Arthur Lynch. Back from left are Katherine Elizabeth Arthur and Jeremiah Dyke Lynch.
COURTESY ANN-MARIE WOLCOTT

OPPOSITE: St. Isaac Joques S.J. chapel, located on Hecker Island in Lake George, was built by Father Peter Moron, C.S.P. COURTESY PAULIST FATHERS

ABOVE: The Crandall Boys Savings Club in the early 1900s. Henry Crandall is seated in the dark suit at center. COURTESY THE FOLKLIFE CENTER, CRANDALL PUBLIC LIBRARY, CLP-OV-103

OPPOSITE TOP: Bayview, the beautiful home of Madam Sembrich, Bolton Landing, circa 1915. COURTESY CHAPMAN MUSEUM

OPPOSITE BOTTOM LEFT: Flower girls at the wedding of New York Governor John Alden Dix of Glens Falls, 1903. From left: Maybelle Ruggs Theobald, Helen Finch Kasson, Eva Thomson and Marion Sherman. COURTESY THE FOLKLIFE CENTER, CRANDALL PUBLIC LIBRARY, CLP-2622

OPPOSITE BOTTOM RIGHT: Esther and Marion Burge of Chestertown circa 1905. COURTESY JOHN JANSSEN

ABOVE: A group on the Sherman Island Dam, circa 1923. From left: Hettie (Brown) Titus, Harry C. Sweet and his wife Louise (De Vol) Sweet. Mr. and Mrs. Sweet were the owners of Sweet's Bakery at 74 Ridge Street in Glens Falls. COURTESY NANCY DE VOL

RIGHT: Girl Scouts swimming in Palmer Pond near Riparius at Camp Chepontuc, circa late 1930s. This was the second camp for the Adirondack Council, and was purchased in 1935 after a 3-day capital campaign. COURTESY CINDY HESS

ABOVE: Girls Scouts learn life-saving skills at Camp Wah-ta-Wah in Lake George, 1929. COURTESY CINDY HESS

LEFT: Clarence Wilmarth promoting the sale of Victory Bonds in Glens Falls during World War I, 1919. COURTESY ANDREW HOLDING

ABOVE: Charlotte "Polly" Thomas Wiswall training her horse at the Thomas farm on Country Club Road in Queensbury, 1928. COURTESY PATRICIA PORTER

RIGHT: Mrs. R. George Wiswall pausing in a cleft of the south opening of Cooper's Cave in Glens Falls, 1932. COURTESY PATRICIA PORTER

LEFT: Camp counselors surround Florence Bromley (sixth from left) at Camp Wah-ta-Wah on the Bolten Road near Rainbow Beach. The camp was Adirondack Council's first and conducted on property owned by John Loomis. Mrs. Bromley was the founder of Adirondack Council. COURTESY CINDY HESS

BELOW LEFT: A gathering of Girl Scouts at Camp Wah-ta-Wah on the Bolton Road near Rainbow Beach, 1930 COURTESY CINDY HESS

BELOW: Maynard D. Baker, 3 1/2, left, and Edwin Baker, 1 1/2, in Warrensburg, circa 1933. Years later Maynard was town supervisor of Warrensburg at the same time his brother Ed was town supervisor of Thurman. COURTESY MAYNARD D. BAKER, SR.

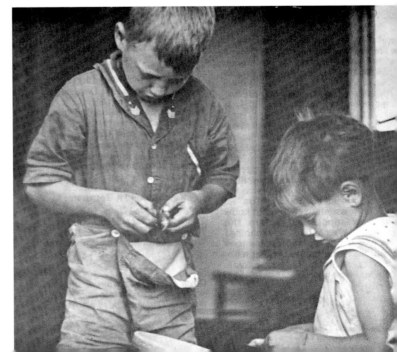

CHAPTER SIX
PUBLIC SERVICE

When the United States entered the Spanish-American War in 1898, *The Glens Falls Daily Times*, later a sister paper to *The Post-Star*, set up an exhibit in the window of O.A. Bower Co. sporting goods and photography supply store in Glens Falls.

An 8-foot map of contested areas was marked with flags to depict which countries controlled which areas. The flags were re-arranged as news from the war reached Glens Falls.

During World War I, *The Post-Star* collected phonograph records from the community and sent them to the Rev. John Lyon Caughey, who took a leave of absence from First Presbyterian Church in Glens Falls to do YMCA work with soldiers stationed at Fort Dix.

Daily newspapers in Warren County have a long history of providing information and boosting morale when local residents went off to war.

Public service also was displayed on the home front by firefighters, police officers and department of public works employees.

Enjoy these historic photographs that depict public service in Warren County.

OPPOSITE: Construction of the Glens Falls city water works, circa 1887. COURTESY THE FOLKLIFE CENTER, CRANDALL PUBLIC LIBRARY, CLP-179

ABOVE: A street sweeper at work on Glen Street in the late 1800s. COURTESY THE FOLKLIFE CENTER, CRANDALL PUBLIC LIBRARY, CLP-1398

ABOVE LEFT: The Citizens Corps in Glens Falls, circa 1890s. COURTESY THE FOLKLIFE CENTER, CRANDALL PUBLIC LIBRARY, CLP-OV-80

LEFT: J.L. Cunningham Hose Co. No. 1 at the South Street Station in Glens Falls, which they shared with James McDonald Hook & Ladder Co., circa 1878. The station was built in 1865 at 38-40 South Street, the same year as the first Ridge Street fire house was built next to City Hall. The South Street Station closed in 1913. COURTESY CHAPMAN MUSEUM

OPPOSITE: Rockwell Corps, 18th Separate Co. Infantry at Camp Farnsworth, East Lake George, August 31, 1883. COURTESY THE FOLKLIFE CENTER, CRANDALL PUBLIC LIBRARY, CLP-121

ABOVE: Members of the Glens Falls Fire Department with a horse-drawn pumper, circa 1900.

COURTESY THE FOLKLIFE CENTER, CRANDALL PUBLIC LIBRARY, CLP-1286

RIGHT: Broad Street Fire Station, circa 1910. Identified are John Mack, Bill Capron and Warren Bristol.

COURTESY CHAPMAN MUSEUM

ABOVE: Glens Falls Fire Department horse-drawn hook and ladder wagon on South Street in front of the Eagle Laundry and the residence of Dr. R. Jerome Eddy, circa 1907.
COURTESY THE FOLKLIFE CENTER, CRANDALL PUBLIC LIBRARY, CLP-790

ABOVE LEFT: View of the Ridge Street Fire Station in Glens Falls, circa 1905. This was also the home of the Firemen's Exempt Association.
COURTESY CHAPMAN MUSEUM

LEFT: A group of Glens Falls Firemen and their dog, circa 1905.
COURTESY CHAPMAN MUSEUM

ABOVE: Warren Bristol in the Glens Falls Fire Department's first motorized vehicle, circa 1915. The vehicle was assembled from a 1909 Buick touring car chassis and box body that held 300 feet of hose. Also known as "little red wood box," a nickname it got at a fire at Finch, Pruyn & Co., when it was used to draw coal to fuel the Clapp & Jones steamer. It was only used at 2-3 fires before being sold. COURTESY CHAPMAN MUSEUM

ABOVE RIGHT: Warren County Board of Supervisors in front of the Halfway House in Queensbury, early 1900s.
COURTESY THE FOLKLIFE CENTER, CRANDALL PUBLIC LIBRARY, CLP-1132

RIGHT: West (Broad) Street Fire Station, July 4, 1914. Members of the department stand with equipment, including: combination ladder and hose truck, the "little red woodbox" (first motorized vehicle purchased by the department), and Babcock aerial ladder truck. COURTESY CHAPMAN MUSEUM

OPPOSITE: Building the Luzerne Reservoir, circa 1915. COURTESY CHAPMAN MUSEUM

ABOVE: Glens Falls Fire Department Engine Co. No. 1 in the 1920s
COURTESY CHAPMAN MUSEUM

LEFT: The Hepburn Library in Bolton, circa 1915. COURTESY CHAPMAN MUSEUM

OPPOSITE TOP LEFT: A view of the busy railroad platform when Company K left for Mexico, June 25, 1916. COURTESY CHAPMAN MUSEUM

OPPOSITE TOP RIGHT: Assistant Fire Chief William Capron in his office at the South Street Fire Station, circa 1920. COURTESY CHAPMAN MUSEUM

OPPOSITE BOTTOM: Members of the Glens Falls Fire Department with their horse-drawn hook and ladder wagon at the Broad Street Station, circa 1915. COURTESY THE FOLKLIFE CENTER, CRANDALL PUBLIC LIBRARY, CLP-788

CHAPTER SEVEN

DISASTERS

Local historians call them the three "Great Fires" of downtown Glens Falls.

In 1864, a fire on May 31 that began in the kitchen of the Glens Falls Hotel swept through much of downtown, destroying 112 buildings and houses, according to the book "Alarm From Box 33: A History of the Glens Falls Fire Department," which the Glens Falls Firefighting Heritage Association published in 2003.

In 1884, a fire on April 28 started at Guildersleeve's Union Hall at the top of Glen Street hill, and spread to the M.B. Little Opera House, and to a row of saloon buildings known as

"Murderer's Row." The fire also damaged the Glens Falls Opera House, destroyed the Presbyterian Church on Warren Street and damaged the Baptist parsonage and other houses on Maple Street.

In 1902, a fire on April 26-27 destroyed 18 businesses on the west side of Glen Street, including that of the *Glens Falls Daily Times* building, and the Joseph Fowler Shirt & Collar Co., which had 800 employees. The fire started at Webb Brothers Clothing & Furnishing Store at 146 Glen St.

Ponder these photographs of historic fires, floods and snowstorms that caused disaster in Warren County.

OPPOSITE: Bridge disaster, March 15, 1890. COURTESY THE FOLKLIFE CENTER, CRANDALL PUBLIC LIBRARY, CLP-1678

ABOVE: Snow piled up in front of the Albany Shoe Store at 85 Glen St., circa 1888.
COURTESY THE FOLKLIFE CENTER, CRANDALL PUBLIC LIBRARY, WILLIAM WALLACE KENNEDY COLLECTION

ABOVE LEFT: A horse-drawn sleigh makes its way up Bay Street in Glens Falls after the blizzard of 1888.
COURTESY THE FOLKLIFE CENTER, CRANDALL PUBLIC LIBRARY, CLP-479

LEFT: Huge piles of snow in downtown Glens Falls after the blizzard of 1888. COURTESY CRANDALL LIBRARY PHOTO COLLECTION AND CHAPMAN MUSEUM

OPPOSITE TOP LEFT: Downtown Glens Falls after the fire of 1864. On May 31, 1864, a devastating fire swept through downtown Glens Falls, consuming the entire business portion of the village. As reported in the Glens Falls Messenger, damages were estimated at almost $1 million. Most business owners had adequate insurance to cover their losses. The citizens of Glens Falls and the surrounding communities had a new fundraising cause and a new tragedy to overcome.
COURTESY THE FOLKLIFE CENTER, CRANDALL PUBLIC LIBRARY, CLP-410

OPPOSITE BOTTOM LEFT: Townspeople gather to view the burned out ruins of the Glens Falls Opera House on Warren Street, April 1884.
COURTESY CHAPMAN MUSEUM

OPPOSITE RIGHT: Bystanders gather in the street to watch as firefighters work to put out the flames at Boyd's Bookstore in Glens Falls, April 28, 1884. COURTESY CHAPMAN MUSEUM

ABOVE: Ruins of the fire on April 26, 1902.
COURTESY THE FOLKLIFE CENTER, CRANDALL PUBLIC LIBRARY, CLP-666

ABOVE RIGHT: View of the chimneys of the Glens Falls Portland Cement Co. after a fire in August 1899. The Glens Falls Portland Cement Co. was built circa 1893. COURTESY CHAPMAN MUSEUM

RIGHT: Aftermath of the Eagle Clothing Store fire,1902. View looking west toward Glen Street taken from the rear of the burnt-out store. Shops across the street include P.P. Braley & Co., C.A. Taylor Shoestore, and Leggett & Peddie. The fire started in Webb Bros. on Glen Street, next door to Eagle Clothing, and spread from Exchange Street to Fowler Alley.
COURTESY CHAPMAN MUSEUM

ABOVE: View of a log jam on the river near Finch, Pruyn & Co., above the Iron Bridge, circa 1900. Notice the three men standing on the jam. COURTESY CHAPMAN MUSEUM

LEFT: Aftermath of the fire on April 30, 1884. COURTESY THE FOLKLIFE CENTER, CRANDALL PUBLIC LIBRARY, CLP-1305

ABOVE: Panoramic view east to southwest of the Glens Falls Dam after the 1913 flood, taken from the west end of the Finch, Pruyn & Co. intake structure, June 31, 1913.
COURTESY LIBRARY OF CONGRESS, HAER NY,57-GLEFA,1--18

LEFT: The destruction of the Iron Bridge during the flood of 1913.
COURTESY CRANDALL LIBRARY PHOTO COLLECTION

OPPOSITE BOTTOM LEFT: Aftermath of the fire on April 26, 1902. COURTESY THE FOLKLIFE CENTER, CRANDALL PUBLIC LIBRARY, CLP-752

OPPOSITE BOTTOM RIGHT: House and surrounding trees in a flood, Luzerne area, circa 1910. COURTESY CHAPMAN MUSEUM

ABOVE: Trees in front of the Masonic Temple and the Church of the Messiah Parish House on Glen Street covered in ice after the great storm of December 18, 1929. COURTESY CHAPMAN MUSEUM

RIGHT: The Glens Falls Fire department battling the 1925 Rialto Theatre and Hotel Fire as a large crowd of people gather to watch.
COURTESY CHAPMAN MUSEUM

ABOVE: A trolley car attempts to make its way through heavy snow on Glen Street after a major storm, February 15, 1914.
COURTESY CHAPMAN MUSEUM

ABOVE LEFT: A view of the Iron Bridge as the flood waters in 1913 begin to pound away at the supports.
COURTESY POSTCARD COLLECTION,
THE FOLKLIFE CENTER, CRANDALL PUBLIC LIBRARY

LEFT: The Glens Falls Fire Department battles the Rialto fire in 1925.
COURTESY CHAPMAN MUSEUM

CHAPTER EIGHT

RECREATION AND CELEBRATION

In 1648, Father Isaac Jogues, a French Catholic missionary, named the body of water now known by the name Lake George as Lac du St. Sacrement, which translated to English means Lake of the Blessed Sacrament.

Warren County residents and tourists have long been blessed with natural resources that provide recreational opportunities, whether it is skiing, tobogganing, boating, swimming, fishing, camping, or simply soaking up the scenery from the porches or grounds of great hotels.

Warren County residents also enjoyed traditional sports such as baseball, bicycling and hunting.

Downtown Glens Falls has long been a gathering place for events such as circuses, patriotic ceremonies, parades and political rallies.

Notable politicians that spoke in Glens Falls included Stephen Douglas, Ulysses S. Grant, Theodore Roosevelt and New York Gov. Charles Whitman.

Roosevelt came to Warren County for fishing, not just politics.

Enjoy these historic photographs of recreation in Warren County.

OPPOSITE: Skiers gathering on Gore Mountain logging road in North Creek, 1933. The group was interviewed by the Post-Star as the first "outsiders" to ski there. Included in the photo are Harold Cutter, Ralph Baker, Gerry Penny, Frank McCourt, Steve Duell, Roy Wiles, George Smith, and Dan Thomas.
COURTESY THE MCCOURT SISTERS

ABOVE: Reception for the 22nd Regiment at Glens Falls, June 6, 1863.
COURTESY THE FOLKLIFE CENTER, CRANDALL PUBLIC LIBRARY, CLP-1335

ABOVE RIGHT: Glens Falls Waltonians enjoying a picnic at Lake George,
August 18, 1870. COURTESY THE FOLKLIFE CENTER, CRANDALL PUBLIC LIBRARY, CLP-168

RIGHT: The Soldiers' Monument shortly after it
was dedicated on Decoration Day, May 30, 1872.
COURTESY THE FOLKLIFE CENTER, CRANDALL PUBLIC LIBRARY, CLP-OV-26

OPPOSITE: Glens Falls Waltonians at Lake George, August 18, 1870.
COURTESY THE FOLKLIFE CENTER, CRANDALL PUBLIC LIBRARY, CLP-169

ABOVE: Three gentlemen out for a ride on a bicycle built for three, circa 1890. COURTESY THE FOLKLIFE CENTER, CRANDALL PUBLIC LIBRARY, CLP-1855

ABOVE RIGHT: Members of the Hi-yoo-skoo-kum Club return from a successful hunt on the Cedar River, circa 1894. Included in the group are Daniel S. Robertson, Rev. Sherman M. Williams, Clarence M. Wilmarth, Captain Ames, Herbert Everest, Doctor Coffin, Frank Gilbert and Martin Wilmarth. COURTESY THE FOLKLIFE CENTER, CRANDALL PUBLIC LIBRARY, CLP-420

RIGHT: View of the Horicon Lodge at Ripley's Point (now Cleverdale) in Queensbury. COURTESY CHAPMAN MUSEUM

ABOVE: Guests on the porch of Sherman House at French Pt. on Lake George, above Bolton, circa 1878. COURTESY CHAPMAN MUSEUM

LEFT: A crowd of people on Glen Street, possibly going to see Gov. Roswell P. Flower on his visit to Glens Falls in 1893. COURTESY CHAPMAN MUSEUM

ABOVE: Guests enjoying their stay at the Hillside Hotel in Hague in the late 1800s. Originally built as a boarding house in 1880 by Lewis Burgess and John McClanathan, the structure was located on Route 9N at the center of town. An early ad for The Hillside noted: "This house is pleasantly situated on high ground, in one of the most beautiful localities of this famous watering place. The fishing is good, and plenty of good boats are kept constantly on hand for the accommodation of guests." The Hillside was enlarged in 1901, expanding its capacity to accommodate up to 80 guests. Thomas Bolton renovated the hotel in 1929, adding electricity and running water, but the building burned to the ground in 1930. COURTESY TOWN OF HAGUE HISTORICAL ARCHIVES

ABOVE LEFT: Boat landing of the Mohican House, Bolton, circa 1880. COURTESY CHAPMAN MUSEUM

LEFT: Boat built in the Sexton boat building shop in Hague to take Smith Sexton's hotel guests on pleasure cruises. It could hold 12 passengers. Smith Sexton built the Uncas Hotel and the Mohican House, both in the Silver Bay neighborhood of Hague. The Uncas Hotel, built in the 1890s, is shown in the photo. It is still in operation today, known as the Northern Lake George Resort and owned by the Martucci family. COURTESY TOWN OF HAGUE HISTORICAL ARCHIVES

OPPOSITE: Children gathered on the school lawn, presumably of Union School No.1, on Glen Street, for a Columbus Day parade, October 12, 1892. COURTESY CHAPMAN MUSEUM

ABOVE: Island Harbor House Hotel, 1896. Owner Albert Clifton is at center of photo (sitting, with mustache). His wife, Bessie, is on porch, second from right. Built in 1882, the Island Harbor House Hotel was located about one mile north of the center of Hague, across from the Waltonian Island group. The hotel originally had 14 bedrooms, but was expanded in 1903 to accommodate 50 guests. It burned in 1933, but reopened the next year in a building on a point of land just to the north of the original site. That building was once the home of Colonel D'Alton Mann, who had built it on the State-owned Waltonian Island. After being told by the State that he could not stay there, Mann moved his house across the ice in 1917 to the point of land where it still sits today. The hotel was sold in 1967 and is now a private home. COURTESY TOWN OF HAGUE HISTORICAL ARCHIVES

RIGHT: Hague regularly hosted a very popular ice harness race, which drew up to 800 attendees. The horses were "sharp shod" with four-pointed metal calks on each shoe to prevent slipping, and the course was kite-shaped. In 1912, about 25 horses came for a three-day series. In 1899, the first place award was a blanket, the second place award was a whip. Later races featured purses ranging from five bushels of oats to monetary awards of $25 to more than $100.
COURTESY TOWN OF HAGUE HISTORICAL ARCHIVES

OPPOSITE: Fort William Henry Hotel on Lake George, circa 1890. COURTESY THE FOLKLIFE CENTER, CRANDALL PUBLIC LIBRARY, CLP-OV-8

ABOVE: The Lake George Regatta Association (LGRA) held the first Hague Regatta in 1888. Rowboats, canoes, naptha launches, and other racing boats competed in these annual regattas, with participants coming from Hague, Bolton, and other towns on the lake. Diving and swimming competitions were also part of the event. The 1914 Gold Cup race was held in Bolton under the auspices of the LGRA. The last Hague regatta was held in 1930, when the LGRA disbanded. In the 1950s, a small group of Hague residents reconstituted the LGRA and held the Northern Lake George Marathon for stock utility outboard racing boats for several years under its auspices. The 90-mile marathon attracted as many as 15,000 spectators and racers came from as far away as Michigan. COURTESY TOWN OF HAGUE HISTORICAL ARCHIVES

LEFT: Horse Trot Poster from 1899. COURTESY TOWN OF HAGUE HISTORICAL ARCHIVES

OPPOSITE: Bicycle club on Glen Street in front of Ordway Hall and Rochester Clothing, circa 1900. COURTESY THE FOLKLIFE CENTER, CRANDALL PUBLIC LIBRARY, CLP-1577

HORSE TROT !

A TWO DAYS' ICE MEETING WILL BE HELD AT

HAGUE, N.Y.

ON LAKE GEORGE,

WEDNESDAY AND THURSDAY,

FEBRUARY 8 AND 9, 1899,

UNDER THE AUSPICES OF THE

-- Hague Trotting Association. --

PROGRAMME—FIRST DAY.

No. 1.—3-Year-Old Race, for horses owned in Hague. Prize, Blanket to first; Whip to second.
No. 2.—For Road Horses owned in Hague, Horicon and Bolton. Purse, $___, divided as follows $___ to 1st, ___ to 2d, ___ to 3rd.

SECOND DAY

No. 3.—Farmer's Race. Purse, $___; divided $___ to 1st, ___ to 2d, ___ to 3d.
No. 4.—Free-for-all. Purse, $___; divided $___ to 1st, ___ to 2d, ___ to 3d.

CONDITIONS

ABOVE: The Wilmarths, DeWolfs, Pecks, and Blauvelts gathering together for a picnic on Lake George, 1902. Back Row: Uncle Will DeWolfe, C.M. Wilmarth, M.L. Wilmarth, Ruben Peck, Mrs. Harmon Blauvelt, Miss Beverly, Mr. Prescott Folevell, Beretea Wilmarth, Emily Afgar, Agnes Birdall-Williams, Maklon Afgar; Seated: Mrs. Peck, Mrs. C.M. Wilmarth, Lou Blauvelt, Mrs. M.L. Wilmarth, Mrs. Charles Bruoer - Aunt Anna, Mrs. Folevell - Pearl Peck, Aunt Maud DeWolfe, Mary Wilmarth, Frank Wilmarth. COURTESY ANDREW HOLDING

ABOVE RIGHT: Labor Day Parade coming up Warren Street in Glens Falls, circa 1900. COURTESY CHAPMAN MUSEUM

RIGHT: Many of the hotels in Hague had baseball teams. The team shown here is from the Trout House, which was built by John Wheeler as a boarding house in 1863. In the 1890s, Charles Wheeler expanded it, converting it into one of Lake George's grand hotels. Tourists traveled by train to Lake George Village to spend their summer at one of the many fine hotels that dotted the lake's shoreline from the late 19th to the mid-20th century. After disembarking the train, guests boarded a steamer for the trip up the lake. In its heyday, Hague had six hotels: the Phoenix, Hillside, Iroquois, Rising House, Trout House, and Island Harbor House, in addition to those in Silver Bay and Sabbath Day Point. Each hotel would send a horse and buggy to pick up guests and their luggage when they arrived at the steamer dock, which was near the center of town. Daily rates were typically $1.50, with weekly rates ranging from $7.00 to $11.00. COURTESY TOWN OF HAGUE HISTORICAL ARCHIVES

OPPOSITE: Friends gathered at Mrs. Bain's Cottage, Assembly Point, circa 1900. Sitting, from right: Mrs. Chas. Carson, Mrs. Jas. H. Bain, Mrs. Horace W. Bell. Standing, from left: Miss Anna Murray, Miss Emerson, Mrs. Norman Sprague, Mrs. Chas. E. Bullard, Mrs. Anna Haviland, Mrs. Chas. Grismer.
COURTESY THE FOLKLIFE CENTER, CRANDALL PUBLIC LIBRARY, CLP-2282

ABOVE: A large gathering for Father Mack's funeral at the corner of Warren and Glen streets, February 20, 1903. COURTESY THE FOLKLIFE CENTER, CRANDALL PUBLIC LIBRARY, CLP-1263

OPPOSITE TOP: Elephants in the Barnum & Bailey Circus parade going up Glen Street as a Trolley emerges from Ridge Street, circa 1905. The Rockwell House is on left side. Signage for "Dr. Haynen" is on the next building. COURTESY CHAPMAN MUSEUM

OPPOSITE BOTTOM LEFT: Luzerne Baseball Team, 1910. COURTESY CHAPMAN MUSEUM

OPPOSITE BOTTOM RIGHT: President Theodore Roosevelt and friends enjoying a successful day of fishing on Brant Lake, circa 1906. From left are Samuel Maltbie, Lawrence Crook, Abel Crook, and President Roosevelt. COURTESY DAVID B. KROGMANN, WITH SPECIAL THANKS TO THE HORICON HISTORICAL SOCIETY

ABOVE: Firemen in vehicles lined up for a parade in Glens Falls in the early 1900s.
COURTESY THE FOLKLIFE CENTER, CRANDALL PUBLIC LIBRARY, CLP-1122

LEFT: Governor Whitman's visit to Glens Falls September 24, 1915. COURTESY CHAPMAN MUSEUM

OPPOSITE: Glens Falls Centennial Parade in 1913. COURTESY CHAPMAN MUSEUM

ABOVE: The Sagamore Hotel, Dalton Landing, on Lake George, circa 1910.
COURTESY THE FOLKLIFE CENTER, CRANDALL PUBLIC LIBRARY, CLP-2842

RIGHT: Martin Wilmarth and family enjoying a day of tobogganing at Glens Falls Country Club, circa 1912. COURTESY ANDREW HOLDING

ABOVE: Glen Falls YMCA gymnastics team under the guidance of Charles Kaulfuss, circa 1910.
COURTESY MCNALLY/YMCA COLLECTION, THE FOLKLIFE CENTER, CRANDALL PUBLIC LIBRARY

ABOVE LEFT: A young boy playing outside his tent at the McCourt Family campsite at Silver Bay, 1922.
COURTESY THE MCCOURT SISTERS

BELOW LEFT: F.J. McCourt Jr., F.J. McCourt Sr. and Bessie McCourt enjoying a picnic while camping at Silver Bay, on Lake George, 1922.
COURTESY THE MCCOURT SISTERS

ABOVE: Elephants making their way through downtown Glens Falls as part of a circus parade, circa 1915. COURTESY CHAPMAN MUSEUM

OPPOSITE: Youngsters at Carpenter's Pavilion in Queensbury, circa 1935. Lake Sunnyside (known as Round Pond, Brown's Pond and Paradise Lake at various times) was popular for its swimming beach and pavilion. On December 4, 1926, Preston and Bessie Carpenter purchased the property. A rumor that a bar might open at the site, prompted the couple to buy the property, so that neighbors and young people would not be exposed to the noise and confusion of a bar. Mr. Carpenter made major changes to the property. He constructed a two-story locker house which he furnished with towels, lockers and Jantzen wool bathing suits to be rented. Sunday was the most popular day for the rental of suits. During the 1930s, dances were very popular, and young women who attended wore long, flowing cotton dresses. COURTESY CHAPMAN MUSEUM

ABOVE: The "Vic Liddle Orchestra" standing under the pergola of the Ft. William Henry Hotel in Lake George, 1926. Among those pictured are J.C. (Vic) Liddle (guitar and banjo), Arthur St. John (Tuba), Donald Curtis (drums), and Donald Hammer. The group performed at various locations throughout the region, from Ft. William Henry on Lake George to the Queensbury Hotel in Glens Falls. COURTESY DEBORAH LIDDLE HALLAHAN

OPPOSITE: The Lake George Swimming Marathon, held in July of 1927, drew 146 competitors from six countries and nearly every state in the U.S. Heavyweight boxing champion Jack Dempsey traveled to Hague to fire the starting pistol. Prizes included $10,000 in cash and valuable real estate as well as cups and medals. The 24-mile course set up for the marathon ran from the Trout House in Hague to the Fort William Henry Hotel. Eighteen and one half hours after the start in Hague, New York City swimmer Edward Keeting crossed the finish line in Lake George Village. Former Hague Historian Clifton West, who was 18 at the time of the marathon, remembered that so many people had crowded onto the platform leading out to the pier that it gave way when Dempsey stepped onto it, sending him and about a dozen of his fans into the ankle-deep water. Dempsey was unscathed, though his fashionable shoes were soaked through. Rule #12 stated: "Any class of bathing suit... can be used. Suits can be abolished entirely if swimmer chooses to use a covering only of grease." Warren County Sanitary Inspector Harry Smith announced before the race that the grease could jeopardize the quality of Lake George's water. The swimmers, however, rallied at the Lake George Courthouse and were able to convince him that the grease was a natural substance (wool fat or lanolin) and would not harm the lake. COURTESY TOWN OF HAGUE HISTORICAL ARCHIVES

VISIT THE
Lake George Area
IN NEW YORK'S ADIRONDACKS

800-365-1050 · VisitLakeGeorge.com · ☐ /TheLakeGeorgeArea

WHITEMAN CHEVROLET

From our humble beginnings in 1956 on Warren Street, Glens Falls... to today, 59 Years later, **Whiteman Chevrolet** continues the commitment to customers, employees and the community, making us a Leader in the Automotive Industry.

In 2011, we remodeled our dealership into a State-of-the-Art Facility at **79 Dix Ave., Glens Falls, N.Y.; Phone 518-792-2196**

We're Your Full Line Chevrolet Dealership and still the "Home of Fair Dealing & Friendly Service."

Lake Luzerne: River Power and the Railway Brought Business and Passengers

Lake Luzerne has within its naming a rich history that extends back before the French and Indian war and the American Revolution. Valleys and hills were occupied by American Indians (Mohawk, Abenaki, and Iroquois) to name a few. At the confluence where the Sacandaga meets the Hudson, a large bay forms and was called ti-o-sa-ron-da, the meeting of the waters. Rockwell Falls to the north contributed tremendous power to the development of the Hadley and Luzerne communities including the lumber industries.

Leather was Luzerne's biggest business during the last half of the nineteenth century. A tannery had been in operation here for some years before the railroad was put through. In 1868 the firm of Thomas Garner and Company, whose offices were in New York City, bought this tannery and immediately an era of expansion began. Thomas Garner's brother, Edward M. Garnar, came to Luzerne to manage the business. Buildings were put up on both sides of Main Street near Mill Street. The Garnar Company moved in at an opportune time, for the railroad had been put through from Saratoga Springs in 1865, and the ease of heavy shipment by rail instead of by wagon was advantageous to the business. Fifty to seventy-five men were employed and in 1887 the Garnar Company bought the Bowman tannery in Stony Creek, where another twenty-five to thirty men worked. E. M. Garnar Jr. managed the Stony Creek tannery and later, when his father retired from the firm, managed the plants in both towns. The Garnar Company's business reached its peak in 1885 and then, after a time, it declined until 1905, when the tannery closed. The buildings were torn down in 1922-23, and all that remains as a monument to a once thriving business is a 100 foot-high brick smokestack.

Further Information: www.townoflakeluzerne.com
and www.kinnearmuseum.blogspot.com

Kinnear Museum of Local History

Garnar Leather Works
Brick Smokestack Still Stands

Passengers and Freight arrive at the
Hadley/Luzerne Train Station

Rockwell Hotel Carriage

Bridge of Hope from
Hadley to Lake Luzerne

Wayside Inn,
Main Street, Lake Luzerne

Garnar Leather Works
on Mill Street

Earlier Bridge of Hope
at Rockwell Falls

Livingston's Inc. is a fourth generation, family owned corporation specializing in home furnishings, mattresses, retail sales and service. Founded in 1901 by William H. Livingston in Gloversville, N.Y., W.H. Livingston Furniture offered goods for the home that included furniture, kitchen and parlor stoves, oil lamps, and various home accessories. Deliveries in this era were made by horse drawn wagon, and day-long delivery trips were common.

Original store in Gloversville, NY circa 1901.

In 1938, a building lot was purchased at 347-355 South Main Street in Gloversville, N.Y. It was to become the new home of Livingston's Furniture. The building was the ideal display space for the latest styles in home furnishings at the time, utilizing hardwood floors and display-specific lighting to accentuate products.

Livingston's opened their second retail location in Hudson Falls, N.Y. in 1959, under the supervision of William B. Livingston. Two years later, Livingston's Quality Manor relocated to its current address at the corner of Dix Avenue and Quaker Road in the town of Queensbury. Under the direction of company president Laurence W. Livingston, and general manager Robert W. Whipple, the store underwent a major

renovation and expansion in the mid 1990's. A grand opening was held in 1995 and showcased the many thousands of square feet added to the showroom floor, as well as the new look of the building.

When you visit Livingston's Furniture & Mattress, chances are you will be greeted by a Livingston or a Whipple, just as generations of furniture shoppers have in the past.

Today, Livingston's Inc. is a full service furniture and mattress retailer that is committed to providing a legitimate option

to the "big box" furniture stores that have become common in recent years. With an updated inventory of today's best brands and styles of furniture and mattresses, competitive pricing, and services that many stores no longer offer (free delivery, set up, and removal), Livingston's continues to strive to be the most reliable hometown furniture store.

In January 2006, Livingston's Inc. was recognized by the Fulton County Chamber of Commerce & Industry as the 2005 Centennial Award recipient. Based on a long standing tradition of great selection, affordable pricing, and service that can be counted on, Livingston's looks forward to being a contributing part of the community for many years to come. At Livingston's, we are not looking for just the sale; we are interested in developing and continuing relationships with our valued customers.

Our business has been in continuous operation in the Adirondack/Capital District region for over 114 years. With over 50,000 square feet of showroom space in our locations in Gloversville and Queensbury, NY, our combined purchasing power allows us to pass savings on to our customers with product lines such as Sealy, LaZBoy, Ashley, and much more.

Stop in to one of our locations today for the best brand name furniture at the best prices possible. Look to Livingston's as the symbol of the better brands at the best prices.

Newest store at Dix Avenue & Quaker Road, Queensbury, NY

At Tri-County United Way, Community Impact is driven by our commitment to the community at large and to our donors. We:

IDENTIFY the tri-county community's most pressing needs.

INVEST your money wisely, employing highly effective resource allocation disciplines.

MEASURE outcomes to ensure that each year's community investments are well-utilized.

Then we report back to you about how the dollars you donate are impacting lives right here in our community. 99 cents of every $1 you donate stays right here in Warren, Washington and northern Saratoga counties!

In addition, we work to address the challenges facing our community by collaborating with and facilitating communication between Donors, Businesses, Government/Municipal Agencies, Nonprofit Organizations, and People in Need.

On your behalf, Tri-County United Way has been investing in the tri-county community since 1923! The result of our united efforts is the unparalleled quality of life enjoyed by all who live here.

LIVE UNITED.

Courtesy Chapman Historical Museum.
Men work in the print room of the Morning Star
newspaper in this photo dated between 1900 and 1910.

The Post-Star Advertising and Editorial Building 2015

O ur roots are deep in the communities we serve. We trace our beginnings to 1904 with the founding of a newspaper called *The Morning Post*. In 1909 the owners of *The Morning Post* acquired the competing newspaper, *The Morning Star*, to launch *The Post-Star*.

For over 100 years we've been telling the stories of our communities. Today our readers access these stories in their morning newspaper, online, and on their mobile devices.

We're proud to have been a part of our history and we look forward to being a part of our future. Thank you for inviting us into your lives each and every day.

THE
POST★STAR
poststar.com

INDEX